PORTRAITS OF GREATNESS

General Editor
ENZO ORLANDI

Text by
HORST HOHENDORF

Translator
SALVATOR ATTANASIO

Published by
The Hamlyn Publishing Group Ltd
Hamlyn House, The Centre,
Feltham, Middlesex
First edition 1967
Revised edition 1969
© 1966 Arnoldo Mondadori Editore
Translation © 1967 by
Arnoldo Mondadori Editore
Printed in Italy by
Arnoldo Mondadori Editore, Verona

THE LIFE
AND
TIMES OF
GOETHE

PAUL HAMLYN
LONDON · NEW YORK · SYDNEY · TORONTO

BORN TO A CHANGING WORLD

Goethe solemnly describes his birth in his autobiography, making it coincide with the ringing of the bells of Frankfurt at the stroke of noon on the 28th of August, 1749. He was baptized in the Lutheran St. Catherine's Church and named after his maternal grandfather, Johann Wolfgang Textor. At that time Frankfurt, an ancient free city, preserved an almost medieval character. Infanticides were still executed in the public square. The world Goethe portrayed in *Faust* was that in which he was born and raised. His later life, however, was to be very different from its beginnings. He saw many things during its long span: wars, upheavals in society, far-reaching changes in living conditions, radical transformations in the sciences and the arts, the reign of Frederick II of Prussia and the Seven Years' War, the American and the French Revolutions, Napoleon's meteoric rise and fall, and even the French revolution of 1830. Further, Goethe witnessed the transition from baroque to rococo and then from classicism to romanticism, alchemy to chemistry, handicrafts to factory-based industry. Hand in hand with these changes was the overthrow of the old theological view of the world. Goethe himself made a powerful contribution to its demise with his belief in a divinized nature. Above all, it was thanks to him that German poetry, provincial in character and meager in volume during his youth, found a European and world-wide reception.

Opposite page, left: Goethe's parents. Johann Caspar was 40 when he married the very young Elizabeth Textor. Goethe always deplored the harshness of his father, whom he criticized for his lack of understanding. He was a cultured but cold man. He regarded his wife as a child to be educated along with the children.

Goethe's mother had a gift for story-telling. She was both gay and practical. She spoiled her "Hans," whom she was to see only rarely after his departure for Weimar. Among the numerous characters created by Goethe in his works we find no trace of his father, his mother or his sister Cornelia.

Frankfurt on the Main in two prints of the time (at left and below). Frankfurt in German means "ford of the Franks." Römerberg Platz, with the adjacent church of St. Nicholas, was the center of the city's life. Every morning, as in the Middle Ages, the guards picked up the keys from the burgomaster in order to open the city's gates.

A FAMILY OF
SOCIAL UPSTARTS

How a descendant of smiths, tailors, butchers and wine dealers became a poet is a mystery. Goethe's family on his father's side came from Thuringia. His great-grandfather was a smith, but his grandfather plied a more elegant trade: he set himself up in Frankfurt as a fashionable tailor. Later, he went to France, where the production of luxury goods was already a flourishing industry. He worked in Lyons until he was driven out along with the other French Protestants by the revocation of the Edict of Nantes. After his return to Frankfurt, he took the name of Göthé. Upon the death of his first wife, he married the rich widow of a colleague, who brought him a big inn, "Zum Weidenhoff," as a dowry. But Frederick George did his most lucrative business with wines, through which he accumulated a good part of the patrimony that enabled his grandson to live in a lordly manner. At his death he left 90,000 florins in lands, mortgages and cash.

His son, Johann Caspar Goethe, did not increase the inheritance. He became a student to fulfill the ambitious hopes of his tailor-father. After obtaining a diploma from Giessen and taking a trip to Italy—an unusual project for a young man of his social class—he asked for a post in the city administration, declaring that he was willing to forego a salary. The city fathers, displeased at such pretension in a tailor's son, rejected him. Johann Caspar replied to the rebuff by buying the title of *Rat*, or Imperial Councilor. This title made him a member of the upper classes, but excluded him from any civic post. At the age of 40 he married the 18-year-old Elizabeth Textor; she did not have a penny for her dowry, but she came from an esteemed family of jurists. Johann Wolfgang was born a year later; other children followed. All but Wolfgang and Cornelia died soon after birth. The Councilor dedicated himself to collecting books, painting, and the study of natural history.

Opposite page: Goethe's grandparents, and a trilingual prospectus of the inn "Zum Weidenhoff," one of the best in Frankfurt, with the indication in leagues of its distance from the major European cities. Goethe's father was born here. The two children in the painting at left are said to be Wolfgang and his sister Cornelia as youngsters.

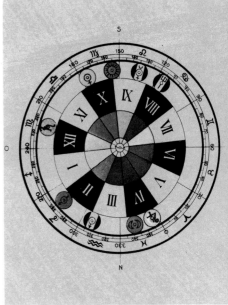

Goethe described his horoscope (above) at the beginning of his autobiography. Two negative constellations, the Sun in opposition to the Moon and Venus in opposition to Aries, according to astrologists, indicate deep conflict: a wavering between the concrete and the abstract, between theory and practice. But Goethe knew how to reconcile these "two souls." Beyond his capacity to resolve the essential problems of life, he had varied interests and views, and was aware of the decisive value of immediate experience. "I have never been affected in my poetry, I shaped only what I felt, what burned in my heart." He was also capable of letting himself be carried away not only by his own feelings but also by the eternal flux of things.

A THIRST FOR READING

Textor, Johann Caspar's father-in-law, was very unlike Johann. A subtle and astute man, he had made his own way in the world, eventually becoming *Schultheiss*, mayor of his village for life. His family were also relative newcomers to Frankfurt, having been there for about 10 years. Textor was a gourmet and a seeker of pleasure who paid little attention to the education of his four daughters.

Goethe was always somewhat snobbish toward his maternal relatives. As an adult he was relatively cold toward his mother, who lived alone during the last 11 years of her life. In one of his poems he claims to have inherited his "vivacious nature" from his mother, but actually he was not a vivacious type. Yet it was from Elizabeth that Goethe got his spontaneity, naturalness, and solid, practical sense, whereas the marked inclination to systematize, theorize and collect came from his father.

He was anything but a child prodigy, but he had a keen intelligence and was quick to learn. In those days no diploma was required to go to the university. It was

Goethe was very attached to his sister Cornelia (above); she was his only confidante and companion. She was not beautiful, having a poor complexion and a large nose. Goethe said that she should have become an abbess. She married a family friend named Schlosser. Cornelia died at the age of 27 when her second child was born. The house on Grosser Hirschgraben (above, left), where Wolfgang and Cornelia were born, had been acquired by their paternal grandfather in 1733. At first there were two houses on the site, which Goethe's father transformed into a single, large structure when his son was five. At left: A painting by J. K. Seekatz, in 1763, depicting the Goethe family in pastoral costume. The cherubs in the background symbolize the brothers who were born dead.

*The festivities that accompanied
the coronation of Joseph II
were among Goethe's
fondest memories of his
youth. At right: The sumptuous
banquet scene in the Römer.
Below: The festive popular
banquet on the public square.
Whole oxen were roasted over spits.
Opposite page, extreme right:
The coronation ceremony.*

enough to be legally of age, and to have attended a secondary school or prepared oneself scholastically in some other way. What counted was a good handwriting, and Goethe lavished great care on his; it remained elegant and flawless all his life. Latin was a basic subject; it was also useful as an underpinning to Greek, which was generally studied with the Latin translation alongside. Goethe learned enough French for his purposes, and also Italian as a hobby. History was studied in the great chronicles, but Goethe developed a permanent aversion to everything historical. He was equally hostile to the religious instruction imparted by the pastor. On the other hand, he was a passionate reader of the Bible, especially of the stories which lent themselves readily to illustration. He had a smattering of Hebrew and English. Drawing was a favorite pastime, along with dancing, fencing, riding lessons. He also tried studying the piano and the violon-cello, but soon gave these instruments up. Above all the young Goethe read voraciously and observed acutely.

GRETCHEN

The first girl appeared in Goethe's life when he was 15. She was called Gretchen, the name he was to give to the heroine of *Faust*. Aside from her name, we know very little about her. Perhaps she was a barmaid or an embroiderer. When he met her, he was friendly with a group of older boys. Goethe had a second house key made secretly in order to meet his boon companions in the evening at the tavern, their usual hangout. This group had taken up the art of forging letters and documents. Goethe himself wrote several compromising letters. When the swindle was exposed, an influential friend of the family managed to hush things up.

We don't know how long the idyll with Gretchen lasted. Goethe, in his autobiography, describes a walk they took arm in arm amid the festive crowd celebrating the coronation of Joseph II. In fact, Goethe managed to slip into the banquet hall, delighting in the splendid spectacle spread before his eyes. It was not the only spectacle that attracted him. During the Seven Years' War, Frankfurt had been occupied by the French. Consequently, it was on the circuit of many traveling theatrical companies from the other side of the Rhine. Goethe attended many of the performances, strolling about behind the wings and the dressing rooms. A passionate admirer of Racine, he is said to have committed entire plays of the French dramatist to memory.

Leipzig, at the time of Goethe's arrival there, was considered a very modern city. Coming from Frankfurt's narrow, twisting streets, the youth for the first time saw a broad city with suburbs outside its walls, and avenues and promenades (directly below, and bottom). Goethe studied drawing at Adam Oeser's art school in the attic of the Plessenburg (below, center). Oeser taught his students that classic culture and ancient statues were the foundation and culmination of every art. Provided with a generous allowance by his father, Wolfgang rented a comfortable lodging (on opposite page, bottom left, the house in which he lived).

RIOTOUS YEARS IN LEIPZIG

The elder Goethe wanted his son to receive a degree in law. So he sent him, at the age of 17, to the University of Leipzig. The young man remained in Leipzig for three years. His scholastic performance was poor. But for his interest in the life around him he deserved high marks. The dramatist Lessing was the rising star of the new generation. His *Minna von Barnhelm*, the first work to usher in a national German literature, had created a furore. The young Goethe, caught up in the excitement, wrote verse and prose, which he was later to burn. He returned to Frankfurt at the end of August, 1768, "almost a wreck" because of the intense life he had led during those three years in Leipzig. He took advantage of nine months of convalescence to become familiar with Shakespeare's works. But Papa Goethe grew impatient with his idle son. So Goethe left home again, this time bound for Strasbourg.

The painting at the left shows Oeser's two daughters, eight years after Goethe's departure from Leipzig. In the summer of 1768 the elder, Friederike, was only 20, her sister Wilhelmina, 13. Friederike was the student Goethe's particular friend and confidante. Goethe did not participate in the usual student life: he did not smoke,

danced little, and avoided quarrels. But he was as susceptible to love as most young men. He learned how to transform a tormenting jealousy into poetry. Käthchen Schönkopf (above) was the first of his loves about whom we know much. The drawing at left is a self-portrait of Goethe in his house at Frankfurt, after his return from Leipzig. The period of calm enforced by his convalescence left him open to Pietistic influences. Pietism insisted on the life of the feelings, demanded continual self-scrutiny and protested against the rigidity of the social order. Goethe drew nourishment from it for his own theosophy.

STRASBOURG

Goethe enrolled for courses at the medical faculty in Strasbourg, chosen for its mild climate and because it was midway to Paris. He dedicated himself especially to chemistry, his secret passion, and to botany. At the inn where he was staying he made the acquaintance of Herder, already a writer of established reputation and five years Goethe's senior. Herder introduced him to the study of the *Volkslied*—folk song. While editing a collection of such folk songs, Goethe secretly included one of his own poems, dedicated to the little rose of the heath. The title of the poem was *Heidenröslein*. With other *Lieder*, or songs, it struck a new note in German lyricism which has no equivalent in other literatures.

These early songs were dedicated to Friederike Brion, the daughter of the pastor of Sesenheim, a town only one day's ride from Strasbourg on horseback. But he soon broke off an attachment that could have no real purpose, perhaps breaking the heart of that poor country girl forever.

Urged by his father to terminate his studies, he prepared a thesis for a degree in church law. It failed to pass the board of examiners because it was too nonconformist. But he did obtain a license that authorized him to practice law. He returned to Frankfurt after turning down an offer to enter the service of France as an attaché to the "German chancellery" in Versailles. Goethe had no wish to bind himself either to a career or to a woman. At home once more, he wrote his first important work, the play *Götz von Berlichingen*.

After spending the first days in the inn, Goethe rented a room in a house on the bustling Zum Fischmarkt (above, left). In Strasbourg he had two revelations: poetry and the Gothic style. Herder (bottom, left) opened his eyes to the poetry of the past: myths, songs, the Bible, Homer and Ossian. (One of Goethe's first acts in Weimar was to propose Herder for a high ecclesiastical post.) Also in Strasbourg, whose panorama was dominated by the spire of the famous cathedral (opposite page), Goethe discovered the Gothic style, which he was to glorify in his German Architecture. Goethe was also influenced by Spinoza (center, left), the philosopher who rejected the dualistic division of God and nature. Spinoza's concept of renunciation was to become central to Goethe's life and work. Above, right: The house of the pastor of Sesenheim, in a drawing by the poet.

THE ROARING YEARS

Klopstock (top, left) the celebrated poet of The Messiah. *Revered by the young Goethe, he in turn complimented him on several scenes from* Faust, *which Goethe read to him in 1774. Lavater (top, right), eight years the poet's senior, was famous for his science of physiognomy, the determination of an individual's essence on the basis of his facial features. Goethe collaborated with Lavater in the writing of the latter's* Physiognomic Fragments. *Later, at Weimar, he broke off*

relations with both men. Above: A Knight Frees a Virgin, a painting by Johann Heinrich Füssl, friend of Lavater and the only painter of merit in the Sturm und Drang *movement. The painting depicts a scene from* The Faërie Queene *by Edmund Spenser, a contemporary of Shakespeare. In October, 1771, Goethe had delivered a famous talk on Shakespeare; a year later he wrote* "Götz von Berlichingen, *a play on the Shakespearean model. On opposite page: Götz in a modern illustration by Lovis Corinth.*

Goethe had his first success, at 24, with *Götz von Berlichingen;* the play was inspired by the life of the knight with "the iron hand," an adventurous captain who lived at the time of the peasant wars between 1480 and 1562. It was dramatized history, a kind of novel arranged in acts and scenes, all power and action. Its coarse and colorful language contributed to its success.

The play was published at Goethe's expense; it brought him fame, but not a single penny. On the credit side, it made him the leader of the famous movement of *Sturm und Drang* (storm and stress), a forerunner of romanticism, around which a group of young people had rallied. They wished to make a complete break with old-fashioned notions, and glorified might over right. The name *Sturm und Drang* was the title of an oversized drama written by one of the group, Klinger, who at first had planned to call it *Wirrwarr* (Hotchpotch). The play was filled with utterances such as, "War, the only happiness that I know!" and, "Where there is fighting, there is space!" When Merck, Schlosser and Herder, in 1772, launched an intensive campaign for the renewal of letters in the *Frankfurter Gelehrten Anzeiger*, Goethe enthusiastically joined them as a journalist. The articles, a collective product of the editors, were not signed. After a year the publisher sold the newspaper, which he considered too militant.

In 1772, in a fresh attempt to make a lawyer out of his son, Goethe's father sent him to the Imperial Supreme Court at Wetzlar for apprentice training. But Goethe did not go beyond registering among the apprentices of that court, where 16,233 cases were awaiting adjudication. Even in Frankfurt, after four years of law practice, he had only had 28 cases. The first dates from February 3, 1772, before the period of probation in Wetzlar. His client, a certain Heckel senior, had retired from his ceramics factory and was now suing Heckel junior for maintenance. The case dragged on until the factory went bankrupt. In the documents, the court deplores the improper way in which the lawyer Goethe expressed himself during his appearances before the bar.

Goetz v. Berlichingen mit der eisernen Hand

"THE SORROWS OF YOUNG WERTHER"

Goethe's first novel, *The Sorrows of Young Werther*, was published anonymously in 1774 at Leipzig. It appeared in two volumes, with drawings by his friend Oeser. The author was 25. From that time on Goethe was "the author of Werther"—until he became "the author of Faust."

The plot is a simple one. Werther, a nature-lover, meets Charlotte and falls in love with her. Charlotte is equally attracted to him. He belatedly learns that she is betrothed to Albert, whose friend he becomes. Werther and Charlotte have one love scene. Then, after a heart-rending farewell scene, Werther commits suicide.

The story of this sensitive youth and his unhappy love produced a fever, as though it had given form to an intimate need of the time. It was as if, unconsciously, secretly, everybody had been waiting for the appearance of that book, permeated with pessimism and racked with universal sorrow. Young men took to aping Werther's dress: blue dress jacket with yellow vest. They committed suicide with a copy of *Werther* in their pockets. Unhappiness became fashionable, love and death inseparable terms. No other work of Goethe was to arouse the effects of *Werther*, so charged with the dynamism of youthful genius.

He had got the idea for the book from his experiences at Wetzlar. At a party he had met Charlotte Buff, the fiancée of a court councilor, a certain Kestner, whom she later married. At heart Goethe was not displeased that she was not free; it assured his own continued freedom. His status of unhappy lover freed him from any responsibility. For him, true freedom consisted precisely in that ambiguous, precarious position. In fact, Goethe fled the moment it appeared that Kestner might renounce his claim to his beloved.

But the greatest stimulus to writing the novel came from the news of the suicide of one of his best friends from Wetzlar, who had killed himself because of unhappy love and wounded pride.

In Wetzlar (scene at left) Goethe fell in love with Lotte Buff (bottom, left). This passion inspired the theme of Werther and the name of its heroine. In the poet's old age, he received a visit in Weimar one day from Lotte, who had the bad taste to appear dressed in the clothes she had worn at their first meeting.

Thomas Mann, in his novel Lotte in Weimar, made this episode his point of departure. The French translation of Werther was lavishly illustrated with engravings by Chodowiecki. Below: Lotte cuts slices of bread for her little brothers (even the real Lotte had 12 younger brothers); Werther comes to take Lotte to the dance; Werther in high society.

CLOSE ESCAPE
FROM MARRIAGE

A friend introduced Goethe to the Schönemanns, bankers who were among the first families of Frankfurt. They had a big house where card games, concerts and balls were the rule. When Goethe made his first visit, a 16-year-old blonde girl was at the piano. She was Lili, the banker's daughter. Standing near the piano, Goethe could not take his eyes off her. After finishing her piece, the girl rose and greeted the guest with the airy grace of a young woman of the world. This Schönemann girl was dangerous: she was neither married nor betrothed.

The mother invited the young lawyer to return. On the other hand, Lili's brothers preferred a rich brother-in-law. Goethe's father also took a dim view of having a lady of quality as a daughter-in-law. But matters reached the point where a betrothal was officially announced. Goethe avoided the binding commitment by going on a journey, a means he was frequently to employ in the future when he wanted to get out of sticky situations. He went to Switzerland with his friends the Stolberg brothers, getting as far as Gotthard Pass. By the time he returned, the wedding plans had gone up in smoke.

Goethe left Frankfurt precipitately; Lili became the wife of a Strasbourg banker. Goethe had let slip by the only chance of a marriage suited to his condition. But it was precisely this that he feared; ever open to love, he was not disposed to love only one person.

Above: An ornamental panel depicting Frankfurt, over a door in the house of Lili Schönemann (left), Goethe's only official fiancée. With Lili, Goethe let slip by the only chance he had to marry a woman who was his peer in terms of social status and personality. The painting (right) by Georg Melchior Kraus shows Goethe at 26 holding a "silhouette" that is said to be of Charlotte von Stein.
A copy made by Schumann, court painter of the dowager duchess Anna Amalia of Weimar, was presented to Goethe's mother, who hung it in her room.

Weimar was little more than a village. Most of its 6,000 inhabitants were peasants, and the style of life was distinctly rural. The castle, which with its adjoining buildings occupied a third of the city, had burned down two years before Goethe arrived. Only its ruins remained. It took 15 years for the duke to build another one. Meanwhile the ducal family was scattered: the dowager duchess had a palace, the young dukes another. Meetings of the Council were held in the ducal residence because the government did not have its own building. There was a domestic air about Weimar. It was an ideal place for a poet who dealt with people, not institutions. The court at Weimar was Goethe's true home, its members his spiritual "family." The painting below is by G. M. Kraus.

DUKE KARL AUGUST

When Goethe arrived in Weimar at the age of 26, he found a court of young people: the dowager duchess Anna Amalia (opposite page, bottom left) was 36, the duke Karl August (opposite, right) and the duchess Louise (center) were 18. In 1769 Anna Amalia traveled to her father's court in Brunswick to present her two sons to her uncle, Frederick the Great. The most famous portrait painter of the time, Johann Georg Ziesenis, painted the king and his two grand-nephews, 12-year-old Karl August (below) and his younger brother Constantin. On the opposite page, above: A view of the new castle at Weimar, rebuilt after the fire of 1774. The painting was done by G. M. Kraus in 1805.

In the early afternoon of December 11, 1774, Captain von Knebel and his companions, the hereditary prince of Saxony-Weimar, Karl August, and his younger brother Constantin, called on the Goethes. Passing through Frankfurt, they wanted to see the author of *Götz*. The animated conversation continued at supper, and since the prince could not stay longer, he invited Goethe to follow them to Mainz for a few days. It was the beginning of a long association, a decisive turn in the poet's life.

Having completed his 18th year and become duke, Karl August passed through Frankfurt again en route to Darmstadt for his marriage. He urged Goethe to come to Weimar. The courts were looking for men of originality, foreigners if possible. Such men were even more sought after if their intelligence was wed to good looks and a vein of gaiety. Karl August had a good eye, and knew that Goethe would be an asset.

Short and thick-set, the duke had a small head, a short nose and a coarse face. His features were more like those of a gamekeeper than of a prince, and indeed he preferred the company of gamekeepers. He also preferred peasant girls, by whom he had a large number of children. He elevated them all to the rank of gamekeeper.

The duke's young wife, Louise, was tall, thin, sentimental, and cold. When she produced a male heir, after a series of miscarriages and girl babies who died soon after birth, the natives of Weimar breathed a sigh of relief. The danger of being annexed to another duchy had been warded off.

The dowager duchess, Anna Amalia, was the dynamic focal point of what was to be called the "Court of the Muses" at Weimar. Wieland, who had come as tutor of the princes, was the first of this constellation. Now it was Goethe's turn. He arrived in Weimar on November 7, 1775.

ELEVEN YEARS
LOST TO THE
WORLD OF LETTERS

Goethe's first months in Weimar were like one big carnival. He soon became a cherished companion to the wild young duke, who had just ascended to the throne and was enjoying himself to the hilt. Goethe, who was still all *Sturm und Drang*, seemed to enjoy this life of pleasure, even if in his heart he could not endure certain coarse habits of the duke: the ever-lit pipe between his teeth, the enormous hunting dogs that he was always dragging behind him, the tedious practical jokes. But nothing disturbed the close relations between the two young men in that free and festive climate. This was not Frankfurt, where an old father disapproved and a standoffish society criticized. Here there was only the good friend who thought that everything Goethe did was marvelous and who moreover was the master whose tastes were beyond discussion. Goethe meanwhile managed to get himself liked even by the dowager duchess. He was an interesting man, and nothing was more feared than boredom in tiny courts like Weimar, where nothing ever happened and where every diversion, no matter how small, was already an event. Goethe published nothing for eleven years. The world of letters seemed to have lost him. He worked only for the "Court of the Muses": he wrote plays for dilettantes and verses for sundry occasions; he organized parties, theatrical spectacles, masquerades and balls.

Goethe visited the Harz mountains region during the winter of 1777. Calling himself Weber, a painter, he was pleased that he was not recognized. He often traveled incognito, delighting in the simple people he met in peasant taverns (above, in an 18th-century print). He also climbed to the peak of the Brocken mountain, a meeting place of witches according to popular superstition. It was to appear in Faust. *It had been a hard job to convince the guide to accompany him through the snowdrifts in the month of December, a climb that was a "first" of its kind in view of the season. At the left: A view of the park at the Weimar castle, painted by G. M. Kraus.*

The drawing by Lips (below), done in 1791, is the last portrait of the young Goethe. In 1782, the poet had become von Goethe: the duke's table was reserved for noblemen, so the duke obtained a title for him in order to enjoy his company at dinner.

Among other posts, Goethe was president of the commission for war. The duchy's armed forces consisted of 532 infantrymen, eight artillerymen and 30 Hussars. Goethe reduced the infantry to 293 men and abolished the artillery, but he kept the Hussars, who were indispensable during feasts, as guards to escort deserters, and as tax collectors. *Above, left:* An inspection of recruits (drawing by Goethe, 1779). *At left:* Four engravings by Chodowiecki: the butcher, the judge, the coachman, the shoemaker. *Right:* three drawings by Goethe: a tower (top); a bridge over the river Ilm with the gate and the garden where his little house was located (center); the valley of the Stutzer River (below). *Opposite page, top:* Corona Schröter; *below:* the actress as Iphigenie and Goethe as Orestes in the performance of Iphigenie *at Ettersberg.*

"IPHIGENIE IN TAURIS"

In Weimar Goethe also busied himself with the court theater. At his suggestion, the duke engaged an actress whom Goethe had admired as a student in Leipzig, the beautiful and cultured Corona Schröter. Besides being a talented interpreter of poetic drama, she was a singer, composed music, drew, knew four languages and dressed in a most elegant fashion. She was given the leading role in *Iphigenie*, a tragedy that Goethe wrote in six weeks as he traveled through the duchy making visits and inspections. The creation of such a lofty, serene, limpid and calm work under unusual conditions can be attributed only to his gift of being able to concentrate all his energy for a short period of time on a single objective. *Iphigenie*, with its noble characters, the peace, purity and candor that suffuse it, its forgiveness and human understanding, is a glorification of every human ideal. When Goethe later transposed it into verse, it needed hardly any revision.

Meanwhile, the presence of Corona Schröter in that minuscule court could only be a disturbing element. Six months went by between readings, rehearsals, parties, and visits of the actress to Goethe's tiny villa. Dissension and conflicts flared: Goethe was jealous of the duke. The duchess, though used to being outshone, criticized her husband. Charlotte von Stein, the poet's former favorite, ostentatiously stayed away from the première of *Iphigenie*.

The production was put together in less than a week. Goethe played the role of Orestes; Pylades was played by Constantin, the brother of Duke Karl August. The whole court attended the première, and two performances were given in honor of guests from beyond the borders of the duchy. Fortunately for domestic harmony, Corona Schröter vanished from Weimar and from Goethe's life once the play was over. Later Schiller was to meet the actress, then 40 and forgotten. He described her face and figure, devastated by time, but in which the traces of her former beauty were still to be glimpsed.

THE POET BECOMES A BUREAUCRAT

Goethe's tasks in the government of the tiny duchy became more burdensome in the decade from 1776 to 1786. He was a minister in fact, but not in name. (He became a minister in name when Weimar was elevated to the dignity of grand duchy in 1815. But by that time he was no longer a minister in fact, limiting himself to being the personal adviser to the duke.) He followed the course of foreign policy and presided over the commissions of roads and transport, war, and mines. He tried to put some order into the administration of finances. The money with which the duke had to maintain his court and finance his trips amounted to only 25,000 thalers a year. Loans were one way of escaping from the financial squeeze. Goethe and the duke managed to contract a loan for 50,000 thalers in Bern during their trip to Switzerland in 1779. On that occasion the poet showed himself to be an accomplished courtier, scrupulous in his observance of formalities.

Among Goethe's duties were long inspection tours, mostly on horseback, to the four localities in which the tiny duchy was divided: Eisenach, Jena, Ilmenau and Weimar, each one with its own autonomous government. In Ilmenau he came upon an abandoned silver mine, and devoted all his energies to a project to put it back in operation. The enterprise reflected a love to which Goethe was to remain ever faithful, his passion for geology. But the mine, doomed to a slow death by flooding, ate up vast amounts of money and gave none of it back. Balzac, another great literary figure who tried his hand at mining, had no luck with his Sardinian silver mines, but at least they were reactivated after his death. The mine in Ilmenau, on the other hand, experienced no revival then or ever.

In Goethe's day, the silhouette
was as popular as the
photograph is today. A
mass-produced substitute for
the costly miniature, it
was the first gift exchanged
between lovers or friends.
Silhouettes exist of almost
all Goethe's contemporaries,
including children and servants.
On the opposite page:
The duchess in the Weimar
park with some of her
ladies in waiting. Left:
The ducal family during a
visit to Gotha. Above: Another
view of the Weimar park.

Below: A view of the Stern bridge. The name derived from the oldest part of the park, which the bridge joined to the castle. Like the preceding views of Weimar and the park, it was painted by Georg Melchior Kraus. Kraus had known Goethe since the Frankfurt days; he had lived a stone's throw

from the Goethe homestead in Hirschgraben. He arrived in Weimar shortly before Goethe, and became the director of the academy of drawing established by Duke Karl August. He executed numerous prints of the castle and of the region. Kraus died soon after the battle of Jena.

THE FATEFUL MEETING WITH CHARLOTTE VON STEIN

The first meeting between Goethe and Charlotte von Stein, the woman who dominated the Weimar scene for the first decade, took place eight days after his arrival. They had already heard of each other. A certain Doctor Zimmerman played the role of go-between. He had presented Goethe with a silhouette of the lady. And he had reported to her the words that Goethe had uttered upon looking at her profile: "It would be marvelous to see how the world is reflected in that soul." This was all very much in the style of the time, woven of 18th-century politeness, amorous skirmishes, gallant intrigues. Goethe was 26, she was 33. Charlotte was the daughter of the marshal of the court, Von Schardt, and of a Scottish noblewoman. At 22 she became the wife of Baron von Stein, grand equerry to the duke. He was an upright man, handsome and well-to-do, who enjoyed the reputation of being the best horseman in Weimar as well as the most sought-after dancer. Charlotte had seven children in 11 years of marriage. She was not a real beauty but what today we would call an interesting type: small of stature, with raven black hair and large, dark eyes. Her husband often left her alone because of his frequent business trips in connection with the purchase of horses. She lived a secluded life in the castle of Kochberg.

The two were brought together by a mutual curiosity; she was more mature, and he was still in the throes of his youthful, ardent enthusiasms. Soon Goethe was spending most of his day at her house, writing, dictating his work to her, dedicating the first manuscript collection of his poems to her. Finally, he became the tutor of her son, Fritz, whom he educated in his own tiny villa. For her part, Charlotte made a mature man out of the young rebel, placating, educating, shaping him. She was the woman who exerted the greatest influence on Goethe's character, channeling his overflowing ardor toward goals of harmonious beauty. The poet acknowledged his debt to her, as his letters testify. Of her feelings we know nothing. The letters that she had written to Goethe were all consigned to flames.

*Left, this page: Silhouettes
of the dowager duchess, the
duke, and the duchess.
Opposite page, left: Goethe
giving a lesson to Fritz von Stein;
right: A profile of Charlotte.
The von Steins lived in the
castle Gross Kochberg (above);
the pen and ink drawing
is by Goethe. The poet spent
long hours there with his beloved.
Charlotte, sentimental but not
passionate, wan and elegant,
was always dressed in white.
In* Iphigenie, *Goethe fused
some of her traits with
those of Fraulein Schröter.*

IN SEARCH OF THE SPONTANEOUS LIFE

Goethe was weary: his governmental chores had become boring and he had broken with his best friends. Secretly he prepared his flight from Weimar. He addressed a letter to Karl August asking for an indefinite leave of absence, to lose himself in regions where he was completely unknown. He never even mentioned Italy. Only his secretary, Philip Seidel, knew his address and his pseudonym: Jean Philippe Möller, painter. On September 3, 1786, at three in the morning, he boarded the stagecoach with a rucksack and a huge pouch as his complete baggage.

This was not an ordinary pleasure trip, but the period of his life in which he was to recharge his energies. What interested him most was painting. He wanted to fill his eyes with light, images, new aspects and dimensions of reality. He wanted to live, to enjoy the sun, the landscape, women. There was a thirst for spontaneity and naturalness in his flight to Italy. In Italy he breathed the atmosphere of pagan life and culture, and felt at home. Here he spent the most carefree period of his life. His *Journey to Italy*, a compilation of extracts of letters and diary notes, was not published until 1816.

"Tischbein's sketch is ready: it shows me in life size, wrapped in a white cloak, seated on a fallen obelisk while I look at the ruins of the Roman countryside. It will be a beautiful picture. I will find a place in it, but the painting will not find a place." Goethe in the Roman Countryside *is the most famous portrait of the poet. Goethe was right: the painting was too large for its intended place. It was sold in 1789 to a German acting as Danish consul in Naples, and now hangs in the Städelsches Kunstinstitut in Frankfurt.*

THE ROAD TO ROME

After passing through the Brenner, Bolzano and Trent, Goethe wrote in his diary: "Here I am in Rovereto, where the language suddenly changes. How happy I am with this language, which I love from this hour on, the vivid language used by all. The sun shines brilliantly, and one still believes in a god." Below: Two drawings by Goethe, the first of Rovereto, the second of an idealized Italian landscape. After embarking on the Brenta (bottom, the port of Dolo in an engraving by Canaletto), Goethe described the trip on the public canal barge "in very excellent company (the Italians are very ceremonious even among themselves)." Goethe first saw Venice on the evening of September 28, 1786.

Torbole: "Now I am really in a new country, in a wholly alien ambience. People here lead a carefree life as in the land of Cockaigne." Malcesine: "It is not possible to express in words the enchantment of this luxuriant coast. The magnificence of the new landscape before one's eyes is unutterable." Verona: "Nightfall is of singular importance in a country in which the day is enjoyed, but the joy of life is experienced especially during the evening. We from the Cimmerian regions do not really know what daytime is. Living in an eternal, gloomy fog, whether it be day or night, for us it is always the same. How much time can we really spend outdoors enjoying the open, free air?" Vicenza: "I have just arrived, but I have already looked around the city and I have seen the Olympic Theater and the buildings of Palladio. There is something truly divine in his drawings. Up to now I have seen only two Italian cities, and I have spoken with only a few people; nevertheless I know my Italians, and very well. For me the Italians are a great, good people." Civita Castellana: "Tomorrow I will be in Rome. When such a desire has been gratified, what shall I have left to desire?" Rome: "I got a good look at Verona, Vicenza, Padua and Venice, and a fleeting glimpse of Ferrara, Cento and Bologna. My anxiety to reach Rome was so great, mounting hour by hour, that I could no longer wait, and I remained only three hours in Florence."

"The gods be thanked that for me Venice is no longer a mere word. I have touched and seen this marvelous city of islands, this republic of beavers. I have also finally seen a play. Today at the St. Luca theater they performed Baruffe Chiozzotte. This, too, is a work by Goldoni; I watched it with immense pleasure, all the more so because yesterday I was at Chioggia and my ears still buzzed with the vociferations of those sailors." On the opposite page: A painting by Francesco Guardi.

TRANQUILLITY AMONG THE NEAPOLITAN CROWDS

After a four-month sojourn in Rome, Goethe continued his journey toward the south. Naples was the largest city that he would see in his life. Naples at that time was three times as big as Rome, with a noisy and colorful street life, into which Goethe plunged with great enthusiasm: "Only in the midst of such crowds and such restlessness do I truly feel peaceful, tranquil and alone; the noisier the streets, the calmer I feel." He also participated in the life of the fashionable society that he had avoided in Rome; the traveler was now no longer the painter Möller, but Herr von Goethe. Among others he frequented the residence of the English ambassador to Naples, Hamilton, who, together with the beautiful Lady Emma, gave grandiose parties in his splendid villa in Posilippo.

Going on to Sicily, the poet undertook an adventurous trip on horseback across the interior of the island from Palermo to Catania and Taormina. Here he resumed work on *Nausikaa*, began in Palermo, which was to remain in fragments like so many of his works. After a stormy crossing he returned to Naples, and then to Rome, where he stayed for almost a year.

In Naples, Goethe met the celebrated artist J. P. Hackert, who painted the view of Naples to the left, bottom. "There's no doubt that the Neapolitan would be a different person if he did not feel himself a prisoner between God and Satan. He lives between the paradise of his sea and the inferno of Vesuvius" (opposite page, top, left). Goethe climbed the volcano three times: "At the foot of the slope we were greeted by two guides. They girded their waists with a leather belt to which the excursionists hung, letting themselves be dragged up the slope." In the drawing above, Tischbein, who traveled with him up to Naples, shows Goethe pulling a horse that had fallen into the water to the bank. He reached Palermo (top, right) by sea: "Without seeing Sicily one cannot get an idea of Italy as a whole. The key to everything here is found in Sicily."

CLASSIC ROME CONQUERS GOETHE

In Rome Goethe saw all the dreams of his youth come true. Everything was as he had imagined it, and all was new. For him Rome was, above all, a great school where he could study the arts of antiquity. He did not see Giotto, nor the mosaics of Venice or Monreale; he neglected the baroque. For him antiquity was the ideal to be imitated. In Assisi he had avoided the churches of St. Francis in order to visit the Temple of Minerva. It was the first wholly intact monument of antiquity that he had come upon. He was to see the first authentic Greek temple in Paestum, where he wandered through the ruins for a whole day, doing the same later in Segesta and Agrigento. In antique humanity he saw realized what he most admired in the individual: beauty, nobility, independence, balance. Thus he arrived at a discovery of the conflicts and contrasts between the subjectivism of the Nordic world and the objectivity of the classic world. "Calm" and "purity" were now to become the inspiring principles of his life. He definitely gave up the idea of becoming a painter; about a month before his departure from Rome, Goethe concluded that he was born only for poetry. In Rome he resumed his plans for *Faust* as well as for *Torquato Tasso*, while he rewrote *Iphigenie* in iambic verse.

40

At dusk on October 29, 1786, Goethe passed through the Porta del Popolo into Rome. From the Gate he took the Corso, which led to the Campidoglio. Below: The Piazza del Popolo and the Corso at carnival time, in a 1783 engraving. On his arrival Goethe went to the Bear, an ancient and modest inn on the Tevere, where the French writer Montaigne had stayed two hundred years before. But he soon moved in with the German painter Tischbein, in whose house on the Corso he enjoyed the company of other German artists. Opposite page, left: Goethe in his bedroom, in a drawing by Tischbein. Another member of the group, Friedrich Bury, did the drawing (opposite page, top left) of the group at work outdoors, including Goethe. Left: One of the more than a thousand drawings that the poet did in Italy: a Roman villa by moonlight.

Below: A watercolor by Pinelli of the Roman Carnival, of which Goethe gives a lively description. Opposite page, top: Maddalena Riggi, the lovely Milanese whom Goethe met at Castel Gandolfo in the fall of 1787. As usual, it was a hopeless love for the poet. At the end of the Voyage in Italy, *his farewell to Rome is mingled with his farewell to Maddalena, who was to marry the son of a famous engraver, Giovanni Volpato. He belonged to the circle of Angelica Kauffmann, who painted the portraits of Maddalena and Goethe (opposite page, center). A child prodigy* and a famous adult, Angelica married an insignificant social climber in London. But he soon died, leaving her free to marry the painter Zucchi and to lead a brilliant life in Rome. Practical as well as gifted, she and her husband did a good business in art objects.

HAPPINESS IN ROME

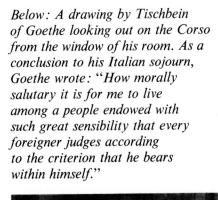

Below: A drawing by Tischbein of Goethe looking out on the Corso from the window of his room. As a conclusion to his Italian sojourn, Goethe wrote: "How morally salutary it is for me to live among a people endowed with such great sensibility that every foreigner judges according to the criterion that he bears within himself."

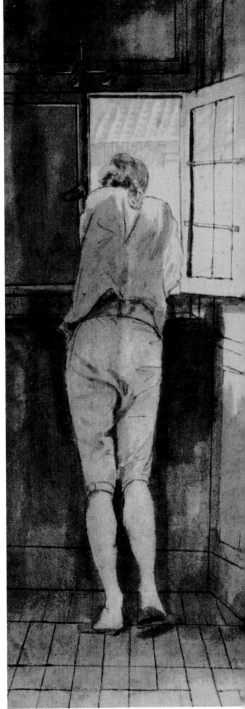

Rome could not compete in size with other Italian cities; at that time it had around 160,000 inhabitants. Hardly a third of the area within the walls, erected at the time of the emperors, was inhabited; the rest held disintegrating villas set in gardens where flocks of sheep peacefully grazed. The person whom Goethe visited most in this tranquil Rome was Angelica Kauffmann. He called her "the inestimable lady." She was famous in London and in Italy as the greatest woman painter of the time, "the poetess of the brush."

It was a bitter moment when he had to separate himself from this pagan and spontaneous life. But he felt impelled to put an end to this holiday interlude if he did not want to lose himself completely. He expressed his nostalgia for Rome by appropriating the utterances of the exiled Ovid in order to voice his sorrow at leaving the city on April 25, 1788. The return journey was swift; from Ancona he wrote to Herder: "I don't know whether I am awake or dreaming as I write you. I am being subjected to a harsh ordeal." The attempt to repeat the Italian experience was to fail wretchedly with a disappointing visit to Venice. Now, from Switzerland, he returned to Weimar for the third time.

HIS "FAT BETTER HALF"

From Italy Goethe had written a letter to the duke stating his position. Upon his return he was to be free of every government commitment. Nevertheless he kept his post in the council and his stipend. This was important because the writer's scanty royalties were hardly enough to maintain his new house. Having given up the dream of being a painter, he was now to be a poet, writer and scientist. He had left Weimar without saying good-bye to anyone, and upon his return he was welcomed as a stranger. Now 39 and lonely, he met a 23-year-old girl, Christiane Vulpius, at the very right moment. She approached him in the park. After paying her respects, she handed him a petition. It concerned her brother, who was in desperate financial straits. The girl worked with two dozen other girls making flowers for clothes and hats from silk remnants. Christiane was a short, attractive brunette, with a pristine mouth and round cheeks, and a low forehead half covered by a cataract of beautiful hair. Goethe took her with him to his little house in the park.

Gossip traveled fast in Weimar. The first to spread the scandalous tidbit around was the young Fritz, Charlotte von Stein's son. She was now almost 50, disenchanted, and thoroughly annoyed. It was not only jealousy, it was the twilight of an idyll: the rather legendary pair of lovers known to nearly all Weimar was no more. The whole of local society shared Charlotte's shock and indignation. A demigod who shares his bed and board with an ordinary woman falls from his pedestal. But Goethe found the relationship convenient; it spurred on his joy in life and quickened his poetic vein. In the *Roman Elegies*, which he now began to write, recollections of his Italian loves are mixed with the image of Christiane. A son was born on Christmas Day 1789; at the baptism, the duke stood as its godfather. Goethe was to regularize the liaison in 1806 with a private wedding. The widow Schopenhauer of Danzig, mother of the gloomy philosopher, was the first to open the doors of her house to Christiane. Others followed suit. In time Christiane's figure rounded out enormously, and people called her Goethe's "fat better half."

Mainz, occupied by the French, was besieged by the allies from the end of April, 1793. Curiosity-seekers from distant localities and peasants from the environs, after tipping the guards, pushed forward as far as the front lines in order to enjoy the spectacle of the bombardment of the city, begun on June 16 (below, in a contemporary print). Top, left: Student demonstrations and rioting in Jena, in an engraving of 1792. In the print to the right: The Prussian artillery at Valmy. The Prussian casualties amounted to 184 dead or wounded; the French toll 150 dead and 260 wounded. The allies suffered their greatest losses during the retreat, due to illness.

"THIS IS THE
BEGINNING
OF A NEW EPOCH"

The French Revolution was a source of torment to Goethe. The romantic of *Werther* who had contributed to paving the way for modern times, had arrived at his own interior equilibrium, which he did not wish to be disturbed. Moreover, his sensual realism distrusted abstractions such as equality, freedom and brotherhood. He fought for freedom, but it was of a spiritual and moral character, not a political one. He was allergic to any form of political enthusiasm, nationalistic, military or revolutionary. His aim was to save mankind with the weapons of reason and enlightenment. But despite himself he was to be involved in the events of contemporary history. The duke, who had taken over the command of a Prussian cavalry regiment, invited Goethe to join him at the camp of Praucourt, near Longwy. Goethe left in August of 1792, with his valet Paul Götz and his secretary Vogel. He saw his mother again in Frankfurt, for the first time in 13 years. Then came the battle of Valmy: "From here and as of today this is the beginning of a new epoch, and you can say that you were there."

The retreat was turned into a disaster because of the epidemics that broke out. Goethe organized his own private retreat, in the ducal kitchen-carriage pulled by six horses. He was urged to write of his experiences, but an old colonel of the Hussars rightly observed: "He's too intelligent. What he could write he doesn't want to; what he would like to write he will not write."

Goethe reached Weimar a few days before Christmas. He burned his war and travel diaries in Düsseldorf. At the end of May, 1793, he was again with the duke. Mainz, which was under siege, surrendered in July. Frenchmen and their collaborators quickly cleared out. Goethe saved one of the latter, suspected of having become rich under the French, from a lynching. And to a British friend, Gore, who pointed out that things might turn out badly for him because of this interference, he replied: "It's just too bad if that fellow peacefully enjoys his ill-gotten gains. After all, I am so structured that I prefer injustice to disorder."

GOETHE AS SCIENTIST

Goethe had a thirst for scientific knowledge. He made his first chemistry experiments as a child, took courses in medicine, and studied botany and geology. In 1784, he made the exciting discovery of the intermaxillary bone of the human skull. Up to that time it was thought that such a bone was found only in animals. Goethe discovered that it existed also in man, attached to the upper jawbone by a light suture.

His scientific curiosity knew no bounds. He once hid an elephant's skull in a chest, afraid the governess would think he was crazy. The idea of an *Urpflanze*, an original plant, came to him during his journey to Italy in the botanical gardens at Padua and Palermo. "All is leaf. And this simplicity will permit the greatest variety," he said in his *Essay to Explain the Metamorphosis of Plants*, written in 1790. That same year, during an excursion to a cemetery in Venice, he explained to the valet who brought him a skull that it really was the skull of a ram. Then he had a new intuition: perhaps the bone of the skull is a transformation of the vertebral column. Nature does not discard its successful patterns. Thus Goethe put himself at the head of evolutionist theories, a Darwinist in advance of all the rest.

He was also drawn to the study of optics, but here his studies were based on illusory calculations and all too little on mathematics. When Newton broke light into colors through the prism, the "visual" man in Goethe rebelled. This was a crime bordering on high treason. Light was one and indivisible, "the most simple and homogeneous entity we know." He fully committed himself to a struggle against the Newtonian light spectrum, calling it a spectrum-phantasm. As a man of synthesis and harmony for whom colors had only an aesthetic value, he could not stand anyone who did not accept his theses, published in 1791 as *Contributions to Optics*. This was followed up in 1810 by *Concerning the Theory of Color*. Finally, in 1820, he published the *Metamorphosis of Animals*, the complement to the other *Metamorphosis*. In both of them he aimed to demonstrate that nature is one; he wanted to show how the variety of forms derives from an original simple and common structure.

SCHILLER COMES TO WEIMAR

Below, left: Schiller and his wife Charlotte. Bottom: Their house in Jena, in a drawing by Goethe. The poet, who was tempted to turn to science, found in Schiller one who listened to him, made suggestions, and urged him not to abandon writing. Goethe, a man dominated by visual impressions and shaped by lived experiences, and Schiller, a man of ideas and abstract thought, had in common their admiration for the ancients. The Greeks' noble ideal of humanity offered them an image of perfection. Schiller adapted Egmont *and* Iphigenie *for the stage. Goethe arranged for the performance of Schiller's trilogy of* Wallenstein, William Tell *and* Don Carlos (*below and center, two scenes from the plays*).

Schiller, the author of *The Robbers, Fiesko,* and *Don Carlos,* arrived in Weimar in 1787, hoping to be welcomed at the "Court of Muses"; but he was sorely disillusioned. Herder was polite, but he had not read a line of his works. As for Goethe, "this man bars the path, and he often makes me remember that fate has treated me cruelly." He observed bitterly: "For doing nothing he spent a stipend of 1,800 thalers in Italy while others for half that sum must bear twice as many burdens." Goethe had him called to the University of Jena in 1789, partly to be helpful, partly to get him out of the way.

Schiller planned to publish a review—*The Hours*—which was to usher in a new era. The best minds of Germany would contribute to it: Kant, Herder, Goethe. Goethe agreed to collaborate "with joy and good intention," but the long discussions between him and Schiller in the columns wearied the reader. The review did not prove popular. The two then began a series of epigrammatic poems called *Xenien.* Theirs was a strange association, totally lacking in mutual trust. But it had a very valuable influence on Goethe, who had neglected the world of letters for so long. During this period he worked on *Faust,* finished *Wilhelm Meister's Apprenticeship,* and resumed *Hermann and Dorothea,* which he composed in hexameters in 1797. This idyll, against the background of the French Revolution, stirred readers. Everybody read it, and the bourgeoisie saw itself reflected in it. All was familiar and acceptable, with marriage as a happy ending thrown in for good measure.

"HERE'S A MAN"

Below: Prussian prisoners after the battle of Jena. Native of a free city and servant of a tiny absolute monarchy, Goethe feared that he would lose everything he had built up for himself in Weimar. He felt that the collapse of the old order in Europe would also sweep away his own position and heritage.

Against Goethe's advice, the duke sided with Prussia against Napoleon, and the castle filled up with officers from the general staff. Goethe, busy in Jena, returned to Weimar on October 6, 1806. On October 14, the cannonades of the battle of Jena were audible, and the retreating Prussian troops passed through Weimar en route to Erfurt. The French arrived an hour after the Prussians. Goethe went to the castle, where the duchess had been left alone, and told her not to be afraid. Goethe then returned to his room on the top floor. Meanwhile the city was plundered.

Two French grenadiers, who had no fondness for bivouacking outdoors, banged on the castle door until it was opened, demanding the owner. Awakened by his secretary Riemer, Goethe went downstairs, offered them a drink, and turned to go upstairs again.

But the soldiers, intent on looting, followed behind and threatened him. Christiane placed herself between them and threw them back. Next day a guard was placed outside the castle gate. Goethe thus witnessed the fall of the world that had allowed him to develop his gifts freely and continuously.

He married Christiane secretly on October 19, with his 18-year-old son August and Riemer as witnesses. But the date engraved on the rings is the 14th, day of the battle of Jena. It was not only an appreciation of Christiane's courage but an assertion of traditional values in the midst of their dissolution. Marriage did not change his mode of life. In the house of his friend the publisher Frommann, Goethe, now almost 60, became sentimentally involved with 18-year-old Minna Herzlieb. The affair was the basis

of the novel *Elective Affinities*, a work that is often wrongly interpreted and is one of his most Christian creations. A couple married more for reasons of fidelity to an old promise than for love is attracted by another couple, the young Ottilia and a captain. The tragic consequences drive all four to absolute renunciation. The plot and characterization revolve around the admonition: "He who looks upon a woman with lust has already committed adultery in his heart." During the French occupation, one of the climactic moments in Goethe's life came when he met Napoleon. Goethe was ordered to an audience on October 2, 1808. "Here's a man!" Napoleon exclaimed as he welcomed him. He talked with him about *Werther*, saying that he had read it at least seven times. "Come to Paris!" was his last invitation.

During the Conference of Erfurt in 1808 (on the opposite page, bottom) Duke Karl August, on October 6, invited Napoleon, the Czar and other rulers to a deer hunt at Ettersberg near Weimar (bottom, right). A deer was placed within a few yards of the rifle of the myopic Czar. The hunt was followed by a grand ball at the castle, during which Napoleon conversed with Wieland and Goethe (opposite page, top). The congress ended with the distribution of decorations. Goethe received the ribbon of the Legion of Honor. Later, Louis XVIII was to confer upon him the gold cross of the same order. Below: Wilhelmina Herzlieb,

for whom Goethe felt a tender affection. Later, she married a professor, but ended up in a rest home, a victim of mental illness. Above, right: Goethe in a portrait by Heinrich Christoph Kolbe. The French rosette stands out among the decorations. The portrait is less solemn than the others executed by Kolbe, who in May, 1822, dined with Goethe practically every day. The poet sat for the portrait after the table was cleared.

On August 16, 1814, the rebuilt
chapel of St. Rocco over Bingen
on the Rhine (below) was
consecrated. Goethe joined
the procession, mixing with
the pilgrims: it was one of
the rare times when he
moved among the people
in a spirit of gaiety and
relaxation. Two years later he
gave the church a drawing of
St. Rocco for the altar.
Center: The ruins of the
Heidelberg castle, in a drawing
by Goethe. On the opposite page,
below: The Heidelberg castle, in
an 1812 painting by George August
Wallis. The English painter Wallis
passed through Heidelberg on
his return from Italy; he
was so taken by the city's charm
that he never left it again.

FLAMES OF LOVE
FOR MARIANNE

In his 65th year, Goethe, while on a journey to a spa
for treatment, felt his soul "full of song like the throats
of the birds along the way" and openly declared to
himself: "Your hair is white, but yet you will love!"
In fact, he loved Marianne von Willemer and was loved
in turn by her. In 1814, Goethe was riding through the
Rhine country in the coach that was his "traveling cot-
tage." In Wiesbaden he was visited by an old friend, the
45-year-old banker Willemer, who was accompanied
by a beautiful woman of 30, buxom and vivacious, with
full lips, flashing black eyes, and thick, curly hair that
fell like a waterfall over her forehead. She was an
Austrian, the daughter of an actress. Marianne herself
was an actress. The banker and senator Willemer had
taken the girl into his house, ostensibly to protect her
from the snares of the world. After settling her in his
villa and providing an education for her, he married
her. The first meeting with Goethe was fleeting. She
had not been married very long. Goethe continued his
journey, making excursions to Bingen and Heidelberg.
He visited the Willemers again in October, and prom-
ised to return. He began to write poems for Marianne,
whom he called Suleika. There were new meetings,
with intervals of separation. In August, 1815, Goethe
was a guest of the Willemers at Gabermühle, the
banker's villa on the road to Offenbach. After a sojourn
in his town house, he returned to the villa on the eve
of his departure for Heidelberg, where he was joined
later by Marianne and her husband. It was their last
meeting. But it was from their correspondence, as from
the "colloquy of songs," that the poetry of the *Eastern-
Western Divan* was born. It was poetry that achieved
the loftiest lyric character. It aspired to be "the most
profound life filtered and enclosed within the smallest
space." Some of the poems in the *Divan*, which for a
long time were attributed to Goethe, were Suleika's.

Right: Marianne von Willemer.
Opposite page, above: A view of
Wiesbaden, where Goethe went
in 1814 and 1815 for the
mineral waters. He met Marianne
on August 4, 1814.

HIS LIFE WAS HIS GREATEST WORK OF ART

Bettina Brentano arrived in Weimar in 1809, when she was 24. Her mother was Maximiliane Brentano, her grandmother Sophie von La Roche, one of the ladies who inspired Goethe to write *Werther*. As a child she had known Goethe in Frankfurt. Indeed, seated at her mother's feet, she had heard her talk about the young manhood of the poet.

Bettina was a dark beauty who was later to become a champion of the emancipation of women. She was enamored of Goethe, and did not hide it. Once she came to blows with Christiane at an art exhibit in Weimar. The fight was stopped by Bettina's husband, Achim von Arnim, who had to drag her away. The poet received a few visits from Bettina after Christiane's death, but even then he was cautious because he knew she was impetuous and inquisitive.

Goethe used a lot of Bettina's gossip in his autobiography *Poetry and Truth*, the aim of which was to make the story of his life a work of art. But an overly broad canvas had its dangers, and a certain consideration for persons of the Weimar circle who were then still living induced him to terminate the work by departing suddenly for Frankfurt. Up to that moment, his life had been a continual ascent. Fate had smiled on him. Everything was reasonably ordered, everything arrived at just the right moment: his first love, his first disappointment, his first success. If at times it is said that Goethe's life was his greatest work of art, it was he who formed this image for posterity: "An event in our life has no value insofar as it is true, but only insofar as it has been significant."

Goethe's wife eyed Bettina Brentano (portrait above) suspiciously; she could barely understand the girl's dialect, but quickly grasped the meaning of her covetous glances. While traveling to Weimar, Bettina had brazenly declared: "I must have a son from Goethe at any price: a demigod will be born." The words may not be textually correct, but after Bettina's last visit, the 81-year-old Goethe made the following entry in his diary: "Repulsed the invasions of Frau von Arnim." After a scene with Christiane, Bettina spread the witticism: "I've been bitten by a sausage with the rabies," which was greatly appreciated by all those in Weimar who liked to make fun of Goethe's fat wife. On the opposite page: A musical evening in the house of the aging Bettina, in a painting by Carl Arnold, a pupil of Menzel.

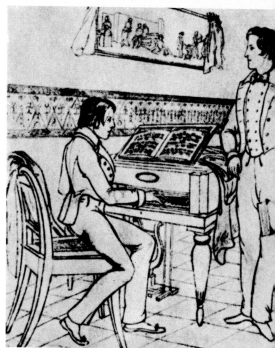

AUGUST IS
BURIED IN ROME

It cannot be said that Goethe's works, pedagogical in intent as they often are, were of much use to him in performing his role as a father. His son August grew up in almost total isolation from him; he was always "the son of Fraulein Vulpius." Goethe waited until the lad was seven years old before he felt the need to make the boy's acquaintance and that of the woman to whose care Goethe's old mother had entrusted him in Frankfurt. At the age of 18, August traveled to Heidelberg, where he was to take up his university studies. On the way, he stopped to see his grandmother, Goethe's neglected mother. The old woman died soon afterwards, on September 13, 1808.

Upon August's return to Weimar, his father had him appointed a councilor of the chamber to the duke, though actually he worked as an administrator and secretary for his father. August turned out to be a lazy, self-indulgent man, addicted to drink. His father began to look around for a wife for him. He picked the daughter of a lady of the court, Ottilie von Pogwisch. Goethe's son looked like a good match to the future mother-in-law, although she insisted that the wedding take place after the death of Christiane Vulpius. This was exactly the way events unfolded, and in 1817 Ottilie became the new mistress of the house. She was soon joined by her sister Ulrike; it seemed Goethe's fate to have the relatives of his in-laws in the house, as had occurred before with Christiane. Two male children were born of this marriage; their grandfather, Goethe, adored the babies. Ten years later a daughter, Alma, was born, dying at the age of 17. Meanwhile the marriage of Ottilie and August went on the rocks. In an attempt to patch it up, Goethe sent his son on a journey to Italy. The departure took place on April 22, 1830; on November 10 news arrived in Weimar that August Goethe had died in Rome on the night of October 27, after a sudden attack of fever. "I knew that I had created a mortal." This was Goethe's obituary of his only son. He locked his sorrow within his heart.

Above: August, Goethe's son. He died in Rome, and was buried in the Protestant cemetery near the pyramid of Cestius at Porta S. Paolo, reproduced (top, left) in an enlargement from a painting by Hackert and, on the opposite page (far left, bottom), in a drawing by Goethe. Left: The poet's two nephews as young men.

Above: Goethe's daughter-in-law Ottilie von Pogwisch with her three children: From top to bottom, Wolfgang Maximilian, Walther and Alma. Walther had musical talent, but no success. Wolfgang suffered from mental illness. Both were bachelors, and died in Leipzig. Alma died when she was only 17.

OLD GOETHE SPEAKS THROUGH ECKERMANN

Johann Peter Eckermann (below) was the faithful assistant of the aged Goethe. The poet engaged Friedrich Wilhelm Riemer (bottom) as a tutor for his 14-year-old son, but he soon became a consultant on all important questions. In his last will and testament Goethe entrusted publication of his posthumous works to these two men.

Goethe's last work, the *Conversations*, was written down by Eckermann, who from 1823 on had been the poet's disciple. Goethe, with an unfailing intuition, had chosen well in this 31-year-old man, who was ready to be subordinate and faithful. Eckermann made notes of their conversations covering a wide range of subjects, all precious thoughts that otherwise would have been lost.

The son of an itinerant tradesman, Eckermann did not learn to write until he was 14. Upon finding a job as a clerk, he continued his studies, attending Göttingen University for three semesters. On the occasion of the 50th anniversary of Goethe's state service, the University of Jena gave him three honorary degrees to be disposed of as he wished: Goethe awarded one of them to Eckermann. He was much more than a secretary. The secretarial work was now done by three other persons: Theodor Kräuter, who was assigned to run errands and make purchases at public auctions, and to keep the library in order; John, a student and friend of August; Schuchardt, who compiled the catalogs of Goethe's ever-expanding collections: coins, ceramics, prints, drawings, rocks, stones, stuffed animals, copies of busts, precious gems. The most important person in this circle was Doctor Riemer, formerly a tutor in the Humboldt household, who was later engaged for August.

After the death of the writers of the old generation—Wieland, Schiller, Herder, Lavater—Goethe reigned as the only survivor of a time that for young people was already history. Many who came on a pilgrimage to him were disappointed. It was difficult to get wise sayings out of him. Faithful to his rule of getting the best out of every situation, he preferred to listen. One evening he invited an inspector of mines from Jena to come and chat with him. The guest found Goethe, Riemer and Eckermann seated at a table, each with a bottle of red wine in front of him, staring contemplatively at some stones: "Stones are silent teachers, they induce silence in the observer, and the best that can be learned is not communicable." In a low voice Riemer told the mining inspector: "His Excellency is thinking." At 10 o'clock Goethe rose and, with his usual words, "I wish my friends a good night," retired to his quarters.

Goethe decorated his house on the Frauenplan (top, left) festively for the 50th anniversary of the reign of Karl August in 1825. At the Congress of Vienna, the duchy of Saxony-Weimar had been raised to the status of a grand duchy; Karl August could then call himself "Royal Highness." The city had been enlarged by almost a third, and now had 10,000 inhabitants. Below: Goethe at work with his secretary. He dictated with great assurance, as though he were reading from a book. He stood up, or paced up and down the room with his hands folded behind his back, his favorite pose.

Goethe and Karl August (opposite page, left) had now grown old. The most popular engraving of the old duke (opposite page, right) is by Schwerdgeburth, done in 1824, showing him in the park of Weimar. He also executed the print below: Karl August returning from the hunt, a scene that his subjects had viewed in real life an infinite number of times.

Caroline Jagemann (top, right) was, from 1797 on, a member of the Weimar theater whose direction Goethe had assumed in 1791. Her close relations with the duke, by whom she had two children, gave her an influence that often hampered Goethe's work. In the face of her intrigues, the poet capitulated, and resigned from the direction of the theater in April, 1817.

FAUST AND MEPHISTOPHELES

Perhaps there is no person in the world whose life is known in such minute detail as Goethe's. We know everything about him through the works that fill 143 volumes, including diaries and letters, and the writings of those who came into contact with him. But if his correspondence hides nothing from us, Goethe in reality tired quickly of such minutiae. He let others attend to them. For he was born to rule, to dominate the scene with his noble and penetrating look. Even his work as minister was really a pretext for acquiring new experiences. Everything he did or saw was an opportunity, a stimulus to knowledge or action. Goethe transformed his whole life into poetry. It is this that gives his works the intimacy and uniqueness that to this day make them appear passionate, young, fresh and modern. He hid nothing of himself, revealing the dual nature that made him both Faust and Mephistopheles. Hence it is no surprise that, in his writings, he contradicts himself constantly. He was neither a systematic philosopher nor a partisan of dogmas or definitive opinions. Although he did not belong to any particular church, he was nevertheless deeply religious. He rejected the exterior manifestations of the Christian religion, but he did not hesitate to assert: "The human spirit will never succeed in surpassing the loftiness and moral character of Christianity as it shines forth and radiates in the Gospels." The writer who more than any other expressed the German spirit was no less acute when he talked about his fellow Germans. "The Germans are a strange people," he wrote. "They make their lives more difficult than is proper with their thoughts and profound ideas that they look for everywhere and apply to everything." But his judgment was even more severe when he said: "The German as an individual is worthy of the greatest esteem; as a group, Germans are wretched. The Germans should be transplanted and scattered all over the world, like the Jews, in order to bring to full development the good qualities that lie in them, and for the health of all nations."

"THE EAGLE
WHO FLIES
ABOVE NATIONS"

Wilhelm von Humboldt

The world of arts and letters fixed its gaze on Goethe. Young Frenchmen went to Weimar with their translations and their homage; Carlyle asked him for a letter of recommendation in order to facilitate obtaining a university chair in Scotland; the young Berlioz, in the letter in which he dedicated his opera *Faust* to the master, corrected "Monsieur" to "Monseigneur," a title owed only to princes of the blood. But if these were some signs of the ever more brilliant radiance of the Goethian light, no less was the attention that he dedicated to European literature, of which he was a passionate reader. Of the French he attentively read Sainte-Beuve, Vigny, Stendhal, Mérimée. At the age of 70 he acclaimed the poetry of Byron with a youthful ardor, attracted more by the personality than the work. He hailed Manzoni as a great Italian poet before he was recognized as such by his own countrymen, particularly admiring his ode on the death of Napoleon. He appreciated good translations, but was aware of their inadequacies and preferred to read the authors whose language he knew in the original. He himself translated many books: *Reineke Fuchs* from low German, Benvenuto Cellini from the Italian, Voltaire's *Mahomet* and *Tancrède*, and Diderot's *Le neveu de Rameau* from the manuscript when its author was still ignored in France. He compared the critical reviews of his *Helena* in Moscow, Paris and Edinburgh, glad to see that German literature was receiving international attention.

For him, "world literature" was the point of departure toward broader horizons, including political perspectives. He rejected every specific national literature because the poet is like the eagle "who flies above nations with a free look." He acknowledged his debt to foreigners: Shakespeare first of all, followed by Sterne and Goldsmith; Tasso and Cellini; the Spaniard Calderón; the Arab and Persian oriental world. He looked boldly beyond the frontiers, in search of new solidarities.

Hector Berlioz

Johann Ludwig Tieck

Thomas Carlyle

George Byron

Karl Friedrich Reinhard

Karl Friedrich Zelter

Felix Mendelssohn-Bartholdy

Franz Grillparzer

Alessandro Manzoni

Eugène Delacroix

Goethe, in Kolbe's painting,
surrounded by two intimate
friends of his old age, Humboldt
and Reinhard, and by some of
his most important contemporaries.
Kolbe, who judged his painting
of 1822 to be too informal, began
this one, which was supposed to
express the poet's nobility
of soul, in the same year.
He finished it in 1826.

"National literature," he said, "does not mean very much now. The time has come for world literature, and each one should busy himself in order to hasten the advent of this epoch." He remained a stranger to Nordic mythology, the German poetry of the Middle Ages, the Niebelungen and other obscure figures. He did not even respond to Dante: "I call classic that which is healthy, and romantic that which is sick" is one of his famous sayings. He rejected systematic classifications in general just as he rejected every attempt to classify his own works. He delighted in confounding his public. It had idolized him as a Romantic after *Götz* and *Werther*. Consequently, after a long silence, the public was astonished by such severe, classical works as *Tasso* and *Iphigenie*, followed about a year later by a new sudden switch to the sensual themes of the *Roman Elegies*. A first edition of these works, in eight volumes, including *Egmont* and a collection of poems for which Goethe had asked 2,000 thalers from his new publisher, Georg Joachim Goschen, left the public cold. His autobiography, *Poetry and Truth*, was to enjoy a greater popularity. He published this work slowly, year after year, commenting on the impatience of the readers, who he intended should be numerous. A careful administrator, Goethe knew very well how to deal with publishers. Celebrated and sought after as a writer, he would hand a prospective publisher a sealed envelope on which was written a figure. If the publisher's offer turned out to be lower, he would not get the work for publication. Today we would call it a kind of private auction bid. In this way Goethe managed to obtain higher fees than any writer before him. He was unwilling to part with the monetary fruits of his success. Therefore he asked for and received a tax rebate in consideration of the fact that he had become "a public person" who daily received letters from everywhere, which he had to answer at a great cost in time and money.

IMPOSSIBLE DREAMS AT MARIENBAD

The spas of Bohemia figure prominently among the landscape backgrounds so dear to Goethe. He went to Carlsbad for 12 years in a row. The first time he went there was on the way to Italy after taking leave of Charlotte von Stein; the last time was in 1820. He did not go there principally for the mineral springs; the cure was more than anything else an excuse for enjoying a serene atmosphere and a society very different from Weimar's. Goethe established new contacts and widened the circle of his friendships at that meeting place of the fashionable European world. There he was introduced to Marie Louise, the Empress of Austria, and wrote some poems for her.

From 1821 on, Goethe abandoned Carlsbad and chose Marienbad as a spa and vacation resort. He took up lodgings in the most lordly and elegant *pension* of the watering place, the Brösigke. It had an enormous terrace and a vast meadow in front, from which, during the promenade hour, one could see all Marienbad and, in turn, be seen. The daughter of the proprietor was a Von Levetzow. Goethe had known her at Carlsbad when she was 19 and had just been married. Now a widow, she was living with Count Knebelsberg. There were three Von Levetzow daughters—Ulrike, Amalie and Bertha. Ulrike, 17, had just returned from a boarding school in Strasbourg. She chatted nonchalantly with the 73-year-old gentleman, seemingly so important a personage, of whom she had not read a line. He presented her with a copy of *Wilhelm Meister's Apprenticeship*. Later, after returning from a stroll in the environs of Marienbad, he brought her some samples of rocks, a hobby that he had never given up. But when the girl's face registered disappointment, he went back to chocolates and wild flowers.

Goethe returned to Marienbad the following year, in 1823. Now he no longer lodged at the Brösigke *pension*, where the duke stayed, but at a hotel called the Goldene Traube ("The Golden Grapes"). By day, the mineral spring was the social center of the spa. Goethe greeted people right and left, and in turn he was greeted and paid deferential homage. He felt young as never before. Thus dreams and projects could come into being in that particular setting, in that somewhat artificial and unreal atmosphere. Perhaps even he, in his heart, felt they were impossible. But what did it matter? This was no reason for them to be less dear to him.

At left: Ulrike von Levetzow; the old poet's last passion was aroused by her youthful charm. Below and on the opposite page: Carlsbad and its mineral spring. Among the many acquaintances that Goethe made there was a beautiful Jewish girl, the daughter of a rich Berlin merchant, Marianne von Eybenberg, who was to contribute to spreading his fame. At this spa he also met Friedrich Reinhard, a Swabian employed in the French diplomatic service. He became a kind of personal observer of Goethe in France, and one of the few friends of his old age. He carried on a voluminous correspondence with him.

Goethe had chosen Töplitz in Bohemia (opposite page, below), for the water cure in 1810, '12 and '13. After careful examinations of the mineral waters in Berka, not far from Weimar, this little town also became a spa on June 24, 1813. Goethe went there in the summer of 1814 and at the end of 1818. Left: Berka, where Goethe met the duke. Above: The Brösigke house in Marienbad, where the poet went from 1821 to 1823. Right: The beautiful Maria Szymanowska, a Polish pianist at the Czar's court, whom Goethe had met in Marienbad and who went to see him in Weimar.

THE LAST PAIN OF LOVE

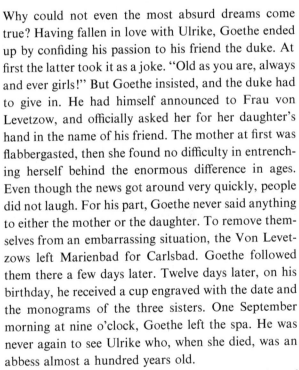

Why could not even the most absurd dreams come true? Having fallen in love with Ulrike, Goethe ended up by confiding his passion to his friend the duke. At first the latter took it as a joke. "Old as you are, always and ever girls!" But Goethe insisted, and the duke had to give in. He had himself announced to Frau von Levetzow, and officially asked her for her daughter's hand in the name of his friend. The mother at first was flabbergasted, then she found no difficulty in entrenching herself behind the enormous difference in ages. Even though the news got around very quickly, people did not laugh. For his part, Goethe never said anything to either the mother or the daughter. To remove themselves from an embarrassing situation, the Von Levetzows left Marienbad for Carlsbad. Goethe followed them there a few days later. Twelve days later, on his birthday, he received a cup engraved with the date and the monograms of the three sisters. One September morning at nine o'clock, Goethe left the spa. He was never again to see Ulrike who, when she died, was an abbess almost a hundred years old.

But the pain was transmuted into an intensity of poetry. He wrote the *Elegy of Marienbad* during the journey. By the time he arrived in Weimar he had already finished his lyric, the most passionate and vigorous that he ever wrote. It expresses the subtlest shades of feeling, without ever striking, however, the remotest erotic note. It was as if the poet had freed himself forever from all that was earthly. Goethe felt and sang each one of his loves as though it were the last and only love. The farewell he addressed to Ulrike is all that and something more. It is a final word, the farewell forever to love, to that feeling that had inspired his poetry and almost guided his whole life.

The Faust and Mephistopheles of the first part of Faust *had a great romantic charm for young people in France. They did not know anything yet of the second part, rooted in classical inspiration, and they were disenchanted upon its publication. Goethe was pleased with the French translation of* Faust, *by the 18-year-old poet Gérard de Nerval. Another edition, deluxe this time, was illustrated with lithographs by Delacroix. Below: Auerbach's tavern. Bottom, left: Faust in his study; right: Margaret using a yarn reel. Opposite page: A scene from Walpurgis Night, in an illustration by the German painter Ramberg.*

THE GUIDING THREAD

At times it is said that Dante and the *Divine Comedy* are an inseparable whole. The same can be said for Goethe and *Faust*, perhaps with even greater truth if for no other reason than that this work occupied him for 60 years. It became the guiding thread and the dominant note of his life. This faithfulness to the themes that he conceived and outlined in his youth, and which he continually elaborated and profoundly renewed, is typical of Goethe the man and the artist. In the beginning, *Faust* was little more than a student comedy lampooning professors and university studies, mixed with the bittersweet incident of his affair with Gretchen. It eventually came to reflect all the spiritual stages through which Goethe had passed and, assuming the grandiose dimensions of a cosmic work, became the essence of his thought.

A similar development is reflected in another great work by Goethe, his principal novel, dedicated to Wilhelm Meister. It was born as a novel whose hero is a stage-struck youth. Goethe's aim was to portray the world of the theater and of the traveling theatrical companies, but little by little the dominant theme became the formation of man, the eternal "apprentice." In the first 10 years at Weimar, Goethe worked sporadically on a first version of the work, *The Theatrical Mission of Wilhelm Meister*, already projected in his mind since the days of *Werther*. *Wilhelm Meister's Apprenticeship* appeared 10 years later, in 1796, and he immediately proposed to write a sequel. He set to work on this at the age of 58, publishing *Wilhelm Meister's Travels* in 1821; he reworked it between 1825 and 1829, when it took its final form.

Goethe, the prototype of old Europe and rooted in its culture, was concerned about the upheavals and radical changes of the beginning of the century. As he began to have doubts about the future of the old continent, emigration became one of the themes of his novel. Although the features of the new century were barely etched, the novel anticipated the advent of the modern and contemporary world. He already had a presentiment of the whole economic and social development of the 19th century with the upsurge of technology, the emergence of the masses, and the rise and conflicts of new classes. It was a brilliant and accurate prophecy.

AFTER SIXTY YEARS HE SEALS THE MANUSCRIPT OF FAUST

"Sixty years have gone by since the conception of *Faust* arose clearly in my youthful soul. . . . Needless to say there was the difficulty of obtaining by an act of the will what should have emerged exclusively from the involuntary workings of nature." These words, written five days before Goethe's death, truly summarize the history of *Faust*. The poet's work lived its own life alongside him, like a creature that accompanied him faithfully to his grave. In 1790 Goethe had already published a fragment of *Faust*, which amplified a first group of scenes going back to the period of *Sturm und Drang*. This was the so-called *UrFaust*, or "original Faust," of the years 1773-75. At Schiller's urging, he resumed work on it in 1797. The first part, finished when Goethe was 52, appeared as late as 1806. More than 20 years went by before Goethe tackled the job of completing his principal work. On July 21, 1831, he wrote in his diary that it was finished. In the middle of August he bound the manuscript of the second part and sealed it. It was to be published in the first volume of his posthumous works.

The tragic story of Dr. Faustus and his pact with the devil had been told for the first time in the 16th century by the English dramatist Christopher Marlowe. Faust signs an agreement with the devil. In exchange for his soul, he will be able to accomplish marvelous works and become the most famous and powerful man on earth. This is the theme that Goethe transformed into a play in which the totality of life erupts. He poured into it everything that had been "accumulating in his heart and unfolding in his mind" in the course of a very long life. In this great work are developed the questions of man's relations with God, the individual in relation to society, the modern mind with respect to the ancient world, and the limits of human potential. With the ascent of Faust's soul to heaven, the poem finally finds its logical conclusion.

Nachtmar (*Nightmare*) is the title that Johann Heinrich Füssli gave to his painting (*opposite page*), which contained all the elements of romantic painting. Nachtmar, *a fantastic being of Nordic mythology, became Mephistopheles' horse in* Faust. *In one of the sketches for Walpurgis Night, Goethe jotted down:* "Mephistopheles wants to bridle several nightmares and lay a trap for Faust." *But he did not develop this scene. On this page: Several scenes designed by Goethe for his* Faust. *Top: A witchcraft scene; below it: The Walpurgis Night. Bottom, left: The apparition of the Earth Spirit; right: The apparition of the poodle dog.*

A WRITER
TO THE END

O'er all the hilltops
Is quiet now,
In all the treetops
Hearest thou hardly a breath;
The birds are asleep in the trees:
Wait; soon like these
Thou shalt rest.

This is one of Goethe's most famous poems, in a translation by Henry Wadsworth Longfellow. Of the many versions of this poem, none matches the original, not because of its content, which could not be more commonplace, but because of the inimitable musicality of the verse. If poetry is untranslatable by nature, this is especially true of Goethe's poems.

On March 15, 1832, the poet caught a cold during a ride in his carriage. The last entry in his diary on March 16 reads: "Spent all day in bed because of indisposition." There was a slight temporary improvement, but later the crisis set in on the night between March 19 and 20. His physician, Dr. Karl Vogel, who was summoned in the morning, witnessed a heart-rending scene: "A terrible anguish and restlessness drove the old man with a precipitous fury now to the bed, now to the divan. The pain in his chest, ever more insistent, caused the martyred man to heave enormous sighs and even to cry out. His features had altered, his color was ashen-gray, his eyes were deeply sunk into livid orbits, tired and opaque; his look expressed the most terrible fear of death. His whole body, frozen, was bathed in sweat." This was followed by a merciful torpor. On the morning of March 22, Goethe asked what day it was. "So spring has begun," he commented, "and we will be better able to recover our strength." A little later he ordered his valet: "Open the blind of the other window, so that more light can come in!" Then he fell asleep again. Ottilie was at his bedside. Awakening at around noon, he wrote with his finger on the blanket that covered his knees. With his last movement he drew a big "W," probably the initial of his name. Thus Goethe died writing.

Goethe's singular greatness is in the absolute naturalness of his development. Spared by a benign fate from the wretchedness of the human condition, placed in a high social position that allowed him to survey all in one encompassing look, and yet close enough to mankind to know the multiple facets of life, animated by a strong inclination to develop his personality to the peak, Goethe set an example as to how life should be lived. His greatest concern was to drive this apex of his being to ever greater heights. His amazing universality of culture, combined with his absolute ingenuousness in seeing and feeling, gave him the power to portray human souls in depth. He hated whatever was forced or artificial, and rejected any morality or politics of an emotional character. For him, morality itself was merely healthy and beautiful nature. He wrote only when, and because, he felt an irresistible compulsion to do so; his is an occasional poetry in the loftiest sense of the word. His numerous sentimental attachments generally turned out to be painful disappointments, but what he found lacking in life he found in a creative ecstasy. As a poet Goethe is immortal, but as a man he is even more so.

1749—August 28: Born in Frankfurt on the Main, son of Johann Caspar, jurist, and Elizabeth Textor.

1756-63—Seven Years' War.

1759—Frankfurt occupied by the French. Friedrich Schiller is born in Marbach, Württemberg.

1765—Goethe studies law at the University of Leipzig, but shows greater interest in drawing and frequenting literary circles.

1768—Afflicted with hemoptysis, he returns to Frankfurt.

1770-71—Goethe terminates his law studies at Strasbourg, where he meets Herder. He meets Friederike Brion in Sesenheim and is inspired to write a series of lyrics to her.

1772—Practices law in Wetzlar from May to September.

1773—Writes his first play: *Götz von Berlichingen.*

1774—He publishes the novel *The Sorrows of Young Werther,* which makes him famous all over Europe. *Clavigo* and the beginning of *Faust* and *Egmont* are from the same period. His betrothal to Lili Schönemann does not lead to marriage.

1775—May-June: First journey to Switzerland. In November he goes to Weimar at the invitation of Duke Karl August, who becomes his friend and patron. Here he finds his ideal environment. He dedicates himself to sundry activities: councilor to the duke, minister, head of the financial administration. These activities, although they are later slowed down, do not arrest his literary activity, nor his study of botany, geology, and anatomy.

1776—Beginning of his affair with Charlotte von Stein, a lady at the court of Duchess Anna Amalia of Weimar.

1778—He begins the novel *The Theatrical Mission of Wilhelm Meister.*

1778—Voltaire, Rousseau die.

1779—Goethe writes the first version of *Iphigenie in Tauris,* in prose.

1780—The monumental *Encyclopedia,* begun in 1751, is published in France.

1784—Discovers the intermaxillary bone in man.

1786—August 17: Frederick II of Prussia dies; September 3, Goethe goes to Italy. Visits Verona, Vicenza, Padua, Venice; barely sets foot in Florence; arrives in Rome on October 29.

1787—February 22: Leaves for Naples, visits Pompeii and Paestum, then all Sicily, then he returns to Naples and Rome. During the happy and fruitful Roman sojourn he finishes *Egmont,* adds several scenes to *Faust,* draws and prepares the pages of his *Journey to Italy,* interests himself in the life of the people, in mineralogy, botany and zoology.

1788—June 18: Returns to Weimar, is exempted from government posts, retaining control only of the scientific institutes and the court theater. Christiane Vulpius, 23, moves into his house.

1788-90—Writes the *Roman Elegies,* finishes *Tasso,* studies the metamorphosis of plants.

1789—The outbreak of the French Revolution shakes his conviction about the necessity of slow and gradual changes in the life of nations, as happens in nature. His son August is born on August 25.

1791—Publishes his essay *Contributions to Optics.*

1792—Follows Duke Karl August in the campaign of France.

1793—May-July: He is present at the siege of Magonza.

1794—Accepts proposal to collaborate with Schiller in new review (*The Hours*). Schiller and he become good friends, the former inciting him to resume work on *Wilhelm Meister's Apprenticeship.*

1794-96—Writes a series of epigrams (*Xenien*) in collaboration with Schiller.

1797—He writes the short poem *Hermann and Dorothea* in hexameters.

1805—Death of Schiller.

1806—August 6: The Holy Roman Empire comes to an end with the official abdication of Francis II. October 19: Goethe legalizes his union with Christiane.

1808—Meeting with Napoleon in Erfurt.

1809—Publishes *The Elective Affinities.* In Ottilia he veils his tender feeling for Minna Herzlieb, who also inspired his sonnets.

1810—He resumes his scientific studies (*On the Theory of Colors*).

1814—His love for Marianne von Willemer inspires him to write *The Western-Eastern Divan.*

1816—Death of Christiane.

1823—In Marienbad for the mineral waters, he is attracted by the young Ulrike von Levetzow, and dedicates his *Elegy of Marienbad* to her.

1828—Death of Duke Karl August. Goethe publishes his *Correspondence* with Schiller and edits the definitive edition of his works.

1829—Last version of the novel *Wilhelm Meister's Travels.*

1830—August, Christiane's only surviving child, dies in Rome.

1831—Finishes writing *Faust.*

1832—March 22: Death of Goethe in Weimar.

The works reproduced in this volume are preserved in the following collections: Dusseldorf, Goethe-Museum Anton und Katharina Kippenberg Stiftung; pp. 6, 11, 12, 19, 22-23, 25, 26-27, 30-31, 32, 39, 40, 46-47, 48, 48-49, 49, 50, 53, 54, 55, 57, 59, 60-61, 62, 63, 66, 68, 69, 71. Frankfurt, Freis Deutsches Hochstift Frankfurter Goethemuseum: pp. 4, 4-5, 6, 7, 8-9, 9, 12, 13, 16, 19, 20, 21, 24, 28, 34-35, 36, 43, 44, 50, 53, 54, 55, 56-57, 58, 64, 68 ,70, 72, 74, 75. Halberstadt, Gleimhaus: p. 15, Marbach, Schillermuseum: p. 50. Milan: Raccolta Bertarelli: p. 27. Rome: De Lemmerman Collection: pp. 38, 38-39, 40-41, 42-43. Venice, Cini Collection: p. 37. Weimar, National Forschungsund Gedenkstatten der Klassischen Deutschen Literatur in Weimar-Goethe Nationalmuseum: pp. 9, 10, 25, 28, 29, 33, 36, 40, 44, 45, 46, 50, 53, 58-59, 59, 60, 64, 65, 66-67, 67, 68-69, 73. Vienna, Kunsthistorisches Museum: pp. 10-11. Photographic credits: Cerasoli: pp. 38, 38-39, 40-41, 42-43, Del Grande: pp. 4, 4-5, 6, 7, 8-9, 9, 12, 13, 16, 19, 20, 21, 22-23, 24, 25, 26-27, 28, 30-31, 32, 34-35, 36, 39, 40, 43, 44, 46-47, 48, 48-49, 49, 53, 54, 55, 56-57, 57, 58, 59, 60-61, 62, 63, 64, 66, 68, 69, 70, 71, 72, 74, 75. Historisches Bildarchiv Handke: pp. 47, 51, 52. Photo Meyer: pp. 10-11. Mori: p. 37. Hans Reger: credits, p. 28. Roger Viollet: pp. 52, 70. Saporetti: p. 27; and the Mondadori Photographic Archives.